Bygone
Helston and
The Lizard

Bygone
HELSTON and
THE LIZARD

Jill Newton

Phillimore

1987

Published by
PHILLIMORE & CO. LTD.,
Shopwyke Hall, Chichester, Sussex, England

ISBN 0 85033 629 5

Printed and bound in Great Britain by
BIDDLES LTD.
Guildford, Surrey

For Frank Curnow, born St Keverne, 1906.
A dear friend who gives so freely of
his vast store of local knowledge
– he is greatly appreciated.

List of Illustrations

Acknowledgements

I should like to thank everyone who has kindly helped me with the material for this book including the following who gave me permission to use photographs: The Royal Institution of Cornwall, nos. 1, 2, 4, 5, 6, 19, 20, 21, 25, 31, 40, 41, 42, 45, 46, 47, 47, 54, 59, 73, 74, 76, 87, 89, 91, 95, 96, 97, 100, 106, 116, 117, 125, 132, 135, 136, 137, 148 and 149; Mr. John Head, no. 8; Mr. & Mrs. K. Oates, nos. 14, 35, 36, 37, 38, 39, 43, 44, 65 and 66; Mr. Ferrers Vyvyan, nos. 23, 24, 26, 27, 28, 29, 30, 32 and 33; Mr. Frank Curnow, nos. 48, 49, 55, 56, 60, 62, 63, 64, 67, 75, 83, 84, 142 and 143; Mr. Peter Greenslade, nos. 85, 86, 88, 99, 102, 104, 105, 107, 108, 109, 110, 111, 112, 113, 114, 115, 118, 119, 120, 122, 123, 124, 126 and 127; Mr. Jan Morgan, nos. 90, 92, 93, 94, 98, 101 and 103; Mr. & Mrs. W. Mundy, nos. 128, 129, 130, 131, 133 and 134; Plymouth City Museum and Art Gallery and Mrs. M. Powell, no. 138; The Marconi Company, no. 140; Mr. R. Lyle, no. 141; Mrs. P. Lee, nos. 144, 145, 146 and 147. My thanks also go to Mr. Frank Curnow, Mr. Douch & Mr. Penhallurick of the Royal Institution of Cornwall, Mr. Martin Matthew of Helston Museum, and Mr. Douglas George of Mullion, for all the information and time they so willingly gave to me. My thanks too, to my husband David for his help in copying old photographs, and my son Daniel for checking my manuscript. Last, but not least, my thanks to Guiseppe and Dinah di Maio who gave me a room to work in when a house move abroad interrupted my preparation of this manuscript.

HISTORICAL INTRODUCTION

The 20th century's way of life came slowly to the Lizard, this remote corner of Cornwall, and most southerly part of Britain. Even now, in making comparisons between the scenes captured in these old photographs and life today, surprisingly little has changed. Fishing and farming dominate, benefiting nowadays from modern technology but no-one has yet found a way to control the elements. Like Celts anywhere, Lizard folk live close to nature; the winter gales and unexpected summer storms bring wrecked boats, lost fishing gear and catches, damaged crops and the inevitable hardships which follow. Yet the hardy inhabitants of the Lizard take it all in their stride; their lives are, as their ancestor's lives were, full of the unexpected and unexplained.

The Lizard is often called the Gemini peninsula, a haunted and superstitious land of contrasts. The western wind-sculpted landscape edged by high forbidding cliffs is in complete contrast to the gentle wooded slopes along the Helford river, where thick holly and oak overhang the water. At some time or another every cliff, cove and quiet inlet has been a silent witness to the last desperate moments of a sinking ship and her helpless crew. Yet the same cliffs and coves on a bright, calm summer's day show only their benevolent and welcoming faces. For this coastline, loved for its unspoiled beauty, has been a cruel graveyard over the centuries. Legends of smuggling and wrecking are as numerous as the tales of unselfish heroism of fishermen and lifeboatmen.

Churches named after little-known Celtic saints testify to the Irish, Welsh and Breton saints who settled on this wild and remote peninsula, the eastern side of which is still called the Meneage or monk's land. There are many chapels too, indicative of the Wesleyan influence, but underlying the strong Christian Church, the old Celtic beliefs and festivals still cling, however unconsciously.

The most famous link is, of course, Helston's Furry Dance with its roots deep in pre-Christian times; a unique festival when everyone enters into the spirit of the day. Houses and shopfronts are gaily decorated with greenery and flowers, the dancers going in and out of the houses, following the old prescribed route, dancing to the familiar tune. By the 1830s the rustic original country dance had been taken over by the gentry and become more sophisticated and orderly, but even today it retains much of its ancient and primitive magic. Originally a pagan festival to welcome the beginning of the Celtic summer on May Day, in its Christian form it is danced on Helston's feast day, the Feast of St Michael, on 8 May.

In the early 19th century the gentry held an annual evening ball at the *Angel Hotel*, and danced down the street to show their finery to the working classes. 'The dancing at the *Angel Hotel* continued with great spirit till the rising sun gave an unwelcome signal to depart.' By the 1830s they had established the Mid-day dance as their own;

'Mr. James Trevenen and Mrs. G. S. Borlase led the one o'clock dance and also opened the ball in the evening'. W. F. Collier, describing a dance at that time, tells us that 'Society in Helleston was divided into three classes, after the gentry danced their dance, the tradespeople did precisely the same with the same band, the same tune, the same dance, through the same streets and the same houses, and after the tradespeople, the working classes'.

By the end of the 19th century the Furry Dance had enjoyed varying degrees of popularity. By 1875 'the ancient festival is almost a thing of the past', just 16 couples danced, there was a servants' party in the afternoon and no ball at the *Angel Hotel*. Luckily someone had the foresight to keep the traditions alive and three years later, in 1878, the ball was held once more. 'The public houses had liberty to keep open all night, and the town was lively to a late hour', although 'Helston Flora has latterly been losing much of its ancient glories and showing signs of the effects of the advanced civilisation of the times'.

How unfair it was, in 1886, for the gentry of Helston to cancel the dance and the fair which was greatly enjoyed by the masses. There was to be 'no street dancing or gaiety of any kind nor will the fair be held' out of respect for a Mrs. Trevenen and Miss Grylls who had just died. Having cancelled Flora Day and its celebrations for the ordinary people of the town, the gentry, who had counted Mrs. Trevenen and Miss Grylls amongst their number, went ahead with their own ball at the *Angel Hotel*. In comparison, when the King died in 1910, the day was only postponed until July.

There was great excitement in 1907 when the Lord Mayor of London, Sir William Treloar, whose father had been a merchant in Helston, visited the town and took part in the Flora Day activities. After spending the night at Mullion, he travelled to St Keverne next day, at the invitation of relatives, to open the new peal of bells in the church tower.

By 1890 the Furry Dance was enjoying renewed popularity and many of the Sunday schools held 'tea meetings' in order to keep the children from participating in such pagan frivolity. Now the Furry Dance is firmly established and with the introduction of the children's dance in 1922 its future has been assured, with each new generation being introduced to the custom at an early age.

The remoteness of the area ensured the old Cornish language was spoken here well into the 17th century. In his book of 1542 Andrew Borde wrote 'In Cornwall is two speches, one is naughty Englysshe and the other is Cornysshe speche'. A century later a royalist soldier wrote that 'the Cornish language is spoken altogether at Goonhilly in Meneage, not far from The Lizard'. Today Lizard folk do not speak Cornish, but I hope they will forgive me for saying they still speak 'naughty Englysshe'. When the Cornish had to accept English as their principal language, some three hundred years ago, they spoke it as foreigners, literally translating Cornish into English and keeping the Cornish structure of their sentences. Even today, Lizard people use the old form by putting 'do' in front of every verb, as in 'he do sing' or 'she do knit'. They also put the most important part of the sentence first: an Englishman will ask 'Are you going to Helston?' but a Cornishman says 'Going Helston are 'ee?'

Evidence of the Cornish language still abounds, for the place-names go back through the centuries. In those early days when people found their way around, unable to read or write, and unaided by maps or signposts, place-names were word pictures descriptive of their situation. Poldhu – black pool; chy an mor – house by the sea; morva – place by the sea; Porthallow – cove at the end of the moor; crousa (crows an wra) – witches' cross. It is a fascinating pastime translating the ancient place-names and seeing if the description still fits.

At the time when photography was in its infancy, life on the Lizard was much the same as it had been for centuries. Helston, the gateway to the Lizard, was an important market town yet it was also a well-established coinage town serving the mining districts to the west and north. No minerals of any commercial value have ever been found on The Lizard peninsula, so the landscape there remained unchanged by engine houses and rows of miners' cottages.

In comparison to the miners who had a life expectancy of about thirty-seven in the mid-18th century, Lizard folk lived long and well. The Rev. Cole, sometime Vicar of Landewednack, died in 1683 aged, it is said, 120, and walked to Penryn and back shortly before his death. Charles Lyttleton asserted he met a man in 1753 who claimed to be 111 and who remembered a dispute amongst Lizard inhabitants as to Charles II's right to the throne. A century later there were two men in St Keverne aged over 100, and more than fifty people aged between 80 and 100, out of a total population of about two thousand. Perhaps this is an indication of a hardworking but well-nourished community thriving on outdoor work.

The farming community had their own superstitions and customs with a strong belief in the power of ill-wishing, even in the 20th century. Canon Diggens, Vicar of St Keverne at the turn of the century, was responsible for recording many small details of local social history. He wrote: 'The office of ill-wishing generally formed part of the duties of the Druid, when two people entered into a contract the Druid was present to utter imprecations on him who should break the agreement. A curse, once launched, could not be recalled. If wrongfully pronounced, then it rested on the head of him who had pronounced it'. Canon Diggens also wrote of a local man who had his cattle ill-wished and had to visit a wise woman in Helston to ensure their recovery. He went to the famous Helston witch, or wise woman, Tamsin Blight, who put everything to rights for him.

At harvest time too, the earth spirits had to be respected, even by God-fearing and church-going folk. The last cut of the corn was gathered into a sheaf or neck, and gaily decorated with ribbons, poppies, cornflowers and yellow harvest flowers. The farmer, his family and workers gathered together on the highest part of the farm, and a poem would usually be recited:

> We must not be mowers, and gather the ripe gold ears,
> Unless we have been sowers, and watered the farrow with tears,
> It is not just as we take it, this mystical world of ours,
> Life's field will yield as we make it,
> a harvest of thorns or flowers.

There was a loud hip, hip, hurrah, three times, then someone, often the oldest lady reaper, would shout three times, 'What have ee?' and the assembled crowd shouted back, three times, 'A neck'. The sheaf was waved about as high as possible. On some of the larger farms there might be a barn-dance in the evening, but usually croust and cider was served to all. The neck was kept in the farmhouse until the following year to ensure another successful harvest. It was all part of the farming year, a custom observed from time beyond memory – a glimmer of Celtic ritual breaking the surface.

There is no doubt that smuggling was rife; fishing boats, some only fifteen or sixteen feet long, made regular trips to Brittany, returning with valuable goods. It was not always brandy or silk, sometimes it was salt, a precious commodity in the pilchard season. In the 1700s, Porthoustock fishermen netted an entire shoal of pilchards, and soon realised there was not enough salt available locally to preserve them. It was at the time of the French wars, and salt was expensive and difficult to obtain. Some of the fishermen set off for Brittany, their luck held, good weather and favourable winds brought them home again in record time and a thousand hogsheads of pilchards were preserved for the benefit of all.

It was said that the honest inhabitants of the Lizard taught their children a unique catechism, 'It is no sin to cheat the government'. Contraband was hurriedly dispersed ashore to find its way into larger manor houses, vicarages, rectories and farmhouses, sometimes for money and sometimes for beef or other goods. One young milliner's apprentice used to ride her horse from Cadgwith, through Ruan Minor and across the downs to Helston and district with hat boxes slung each side of her saddle. No-one suspected her, yet the boxes contained not hats but smuggled goods.

A letter dated 29 October 1803 petitioning for a customs and excise boat at Coverack reflects an increased amount of smuggling at this time, shortly after the Treaty of Amiens and the end of the war with France. The writer pointed out that Porthoustock, Porthallow, Coverack, Cadgwith and Landewednack had no revenue officer and that 'in each of these said coves an illicit trade for Spirits, Tea, Tobacco, Snuff, Salt and etc. is carried on to an extent almost beyond conception'.

It is interesting to see how many fishermen never really needed to claim parish relief, even in the hardest of winters. Men such as John Carlyon of Coverack took their boats regularly across to Roscoff, a three-day round trip, given fair weather. On the third day Carlyon's wife hung his red shirt on the line if the coast was clear; if not, the line remained empty. The signal was also understood by the locals, and when darkness fell and John Carlyon slipped quietly into the cove, his customers were already there quickly to collect and disperse the cargo. From this small beginning, John Carlyon's trade grew, until he owned a larger merchant vessel and traded as far afield as Spain.

The smugglers were not without humour; in the autumn of 1840, 126 ankers of contraband spirit were seized at Coverack and taken to the custom-house at Gweek. On this occasion, with many disappointed customers, the Coverack men engaged in a little 'second wrecking', by marching to Gweek, surprising the guard and removing their kegs. But to keep the customs men happy, they left three kegs for them.

As for wreckers, this was and still is considered an honourable pastime. Just a couple of years ago, a valuable deck cargo of wood was washed ashore early on a winter's evening at the height of a gale. Despite the foul weather, there were a lot of people abroad that night, and by the time daylight came, barely a plank of wood was to be found anywhere on the coast, but a good many barns and garages were piled high.

Apart from the minority of instances, wreckers did not set out deliberately to cause a wreck. A combination of sudden gales and the rocky coastline was sufficient for their needs. Nevertheless, it is easy to understand the reasons behind local opposition to plans for a Lizard lighthouse in the 16th century, on the grounds that it would 'take away God's grace' and prevent shipwrecks.

In those days, long before lifeboats were provided, it was the fishermen who took their own small boats out, often rowing through tremendous waves without any thought for their own safety, in an attempt to save lives. That done, they turned their efforts to claiming the reward by salvaging cargo, timbers, and sails. Strictly speaking, anything they rescued had to be handed in to the customs or coastguard officers, to be sold by auction at a later date, when they received a percentage of the price. Sometimes however, the item itself was more useful than money, so wreckers were 'as honest as it is practical to be'. Any salvaged item moved ashore above the high water line was generally acknowledged to belong to someone else, and left well alone. But there were a few unscrupulous people who would take anything and this was known as 'second wrecking' which was thought to be most disreputable.

Such was the occasion after the wreck of the *Mosel* which carried a cargo of luxury items. Customs officers were concerned that so many people were out wrecking, but not much was being handed in. A house-to-house search was arranged, but the cove dwellers had anticipated this move, and the goods were in various secret places out in the surrounding countryside. They were quite indignant, as they explained to the customs officers that the reason for the heavy losses was because of all the second wrecking by people living up on the downs, a very dishonourable and unprofessional job. But even today many cove cottages boast china and other items from the wreck of the *Mosel*.

Lizard wreckers applied their own moral standards to the job in hand and, on one occasion, they were the losers. Before the last war, a ship went aground at Coverack, and a firm of Penzance ship breakers were working the wreck. The team returned to Penzance on the Saturday evening and came back on Monday morning to find all their cutting and lifting gear had been stolen from the wreck. The police were called in and the stolen items were soon recovered, for the simple reason that they knew these would be close at hand. Although it was quite permissible to go wrecking on a Sunday, it would have been unforgivable to drive a lorry.

There was always rivalry between each tiny hamlet, cove or village. When a St Keverne lass married a Coverack man, at the turn of the century, it was a great loss to her family, for in their eyes she had married a foreigner. Cadgwith men were said to be descended from the survivors of a Spanish wreck, one of the Armada fleet; even now, Jose a is not uncommon name in the area. Today, as always, there is a great deal of competition between the coves, each cove having an annual regatta with emphasis on rowing events. In the days when many of the photographs in this book were taken, fishermen and lifeboatmen depended on oars and their own ability to use them well.

Nowadays when a lifeboat goes out in gale force winds, it has just one advantage over the strong and violent waves, a powerful engine, but think back to the days when a lifeboat had to be rowed out. At the time of the centenary of The Lizard Lifeboat Station, F. G. Chapman wrote,

They are the sort of men who know what it means to be afloat in a small boat in a storm and heavy seas of such severity that large vessels are forced to seek shelter; who have experienced the awe-inspiring sight of huge waves towering above, when the boat is in the trough, and have been made aware of the power of the waves when their impact makes the stout boat hesitate and shudder. They are men wet to the skin from the constant lashing of wind-driven spray, the fatigue resulting from hours of battering by the waves and loss of sleep, and yet remain sufficiently calm and resolute, to take their boat close to a sinking ship, rolling and heaving in the open sea, or amongst rocks and breakers to a stranded ship, and so take the crew to safety.

The first Lizard lifeboat, the *Anna Maria*, capsized on exercise, and three of her crew drowned, including the coxswain Peter Mitchell. A new boat, also called the *Anna Maria*, was soon provided and former second coxswain James Rowe was put in command. With typical unselfishness, the other six survivors of the original crew immediately volunteered for service. Even now, when tragedy strikes a lifeboat station, as it did at Penlee a few years ago, there is never a shortage of volunteers for the crew, and more often than not the same surnames appear through the decades, for lifeboat service is a tradition of honour.

When the emigrant ship, the *John*, was wrecked on the outer rocks of the Manacle Reef in May 1855, it was the local fishermen who went to the rescue. James Hill, a fisherman, told the inquest how he organised two fishing boats to go in search of survivors, of the great difficulty they had in getting out of the cove, and how they finally succeeded in making three trips, saving about fifty lives, but 193 men, women and children were lost. 'The shore was a sight never the be forgotten. One hundred children had sailed in the *John* and side by side in a long row numbers of these little ones were laid waiting identification'. James Hill was one of the first to volunteer as a crew member when a lifeboat was provided for Porthoustock, and was coxswain for many years.

The pilchard industry involved the whole village in the season. The lookout, or huer, on the cliff, scanned the sea from morning till night, always searching for the tell-tale signs that the fish were coming in. He would give a great shout and the entire village would jump to action, for just one good catch would see their families fed and provided for through the winter months. Understandably, when the Cadgwith huer cried 'Hevva' just as a funeral procession was walking through the village, the bearers left the coffin, as did most of the mourners, in a race to get the boats launched and out to sea. The funeral could wait another day, but the fish would be gone, perhaps not to return.

The fish were brought ashore to be packed into barrels, salted and pressed before being sent to France and Italy where they were considered a great delicacy. The fishermen's families would all have a great earthenware pot or bussa filled with a store for the winter. Even the foul smelling oil wasn't wasted: a small container of oil with a wick floating in it was used to provide light in the tiny cottages.

Minerals were never found in any marketable quantity on the Lizard, but a couple of small mines were worked on Goonhilly, for a short period. Even so, with the poor fishing seasons and disastrous harvests of a century or so ago, many of the more adventurous folk left their families and homes in order to journey overseas, attracted by farming opportunities in the new world.

During the 18th and 19th centuries, Gweek must have been a cosmopolitan trading post, with large sailing schooners from Scandinavia, Germany, Holland and Ireland lying alongside Medway and Thames barges and other smaller trading vessels. As less and less timber was needed in the mines, Gweek saw more and more sailing ships taking people off to the colonies. Later motor vessels brought cement, wood, coal, limestone and grain, a trade which continued until the last war. Sometimes it is difficult to imagine Gweek as a busy port. The following description was written in 1890: 'at low tide, the impression is given that the craft have been stranded for years, and it seems strange they could manage to penetrate so far inland'.

Of the large estates on the peninsula, there were few that have made a permanent impression. Bonython, and the family of the same name, is recorded in the area from the 13th century. Part of the house dates from the 1600s and it was from this spot that Captain Richard Bonython left to open up new territory in Saco, America, in 1631. An early settler in this new country, he became an able and efficient magistrate. Not so his son John, whose name appears in court records in 1635 and 1640, including a fine for disorderly conduct in his own father's house. He was later declared an outlaw of Saco Colony and Massachusetts, and took to living as an Indian. The poet John Greenleaf Whittier wrote:

> 'a low, lean, swarthy man is he,
> with blanket garb and buskined knee,
> and nought of English fashion on,
> for he hates the race from whence he sprung,
> and couches his words in the Indian tongue'.

Another estate, Bochym, has changed hands many times over the years. One owner was beheaded, and another, Christopher Bellot, lost his six daughters from smallpox. In 1851, a tunnel was discovered leading down towards Mullion, presumably used for smuggling purposes.

Largest of all, Trelowarren, on the edge of Goonhilly, has been home to the Vyvyan family for more than 550 years. It is said that a Vyvyan escaped on horseback from Lyonesse as it disappeared under the sea, and the family crest depicts a saddled and bridled horse. Until earlier this century, it was a tradition to keep a saddled horse always in readiness. Before the family settled here, they lived at St Buryan where they are on record for assault, wrecking and murder. Later Vyvyans were staunch Royalists; one Richard Vyvyan was knighted by Charles I in 1636. Through the 18th and 19th centuries the house was extended and the gardens landscaped.

Tremayne quay was purposely built in 1846 for a proposed visit by Queen Victoria when she undertook a cruise of the Cornish coast. Unfortunately the weather became unsettled, and the Queen did not undertake the long-planned trip up the river to Tremayne. The marble head of the Queen which was sent by way of compensation did little to relieve the great disappointment. In 1921, the then Prince of Wales, later the Duke of Windsor, landed at Tremayne quay to be greeted by Sir Courtenay Vyvyan, and was said to be very impressed by the lovely walk through the woods. At this time the estate was a self-sufficient community employing farmworkers, domestic staff, gardeners and staff to operate the huge cider press. With changing methods of farming and the introduction of new machinery, fewer hands were needed, and some of the estate workers, whose families had served the Vyvyans for generations, felt the need to emigrate.

There was never much employment in the area other than fishing and farming. In the immediate area around Landewednack and the Lizard, the serpentine workers put the local stone to good use, creating bowls, vases and other small decorative items which were highly prized by the growing number of tourists. The Poltesco works made larger items beyond the scope of the cottage workshops; shop fronts and ornate fireplace surrounds for the London markets. Sadly, an uninsured vessel carrying a large and valuable cargo of serpentine goods was wrecked and the consequent financial loss to the firm led to the closure of the works in 1897.

The quarries around St Keverne were developed and the special loading bay was constructed at Porthoustock to facilitate the loading of roadstone into waiting ships and barges.

Withies in the valleys leading down to the coves were constantly gathered for making lobster pots and thatching spars. The farmland is fertile, the summer season long, and with the introduction of a train service through to London, many landowners turned to the cultivation of flowers, such as daffodils and anemones. Sheltered valleys were obvious sites for the creation of beautiful sub-tropical gardens, as at Bochym, Trenoweth and Bosahan, where exotic species were planted alongside indigenous ferns and shrubs.

Porthleven was the busiest port around this part of the southern coast, and on a Sunday, when no fisherman dared to go to sea, it was possible to walk from one side of the harbour to the other, across the decks of boats. Understandably there were boatbuilders kept in work here with the construction and repair of the local fleet. Some of the Porthleven boats sailed up to the Scottish fishing grounds each autumn to take part in the herring fishery. Many of the Porthleven crews were Methodist and, even when under sail for Scottish waters, they would put into port on a Saturday night, so as not to be at sea on a Sunday, even if it meant missing a favourable wind.

Holidaymakers were soon discovering the quiet coves and fishing villages. Mrs. Craik, from Kent, authoress of *John Halifax, Gentleman*, wrote a very readable and timeless book about her holiday at The Lizard in 1880, much of which she would still recognise today. She took tea with Miss Mary Mundy at the *Old Inn*, Mullion, walked to Kynance along the double hedge path and visited Poltesco as well as other serpentine works. She also made a couple of boat trips with John Curgenven, a fisherman and serpentine worker, who told her about the wrecks and rescues around the coast. Noted artist Charles Napier Hemy illustrated her book with delightful drawings of Cadgwith, Mullion and The Lizard.

Other artists have been tempted to stay and work here too; Arthur Rackham, Augustus John, Henry Scott Tuke and, more recently, John Tunnard who lived at Cadgwith. Resident at The Lizard was Thomas Hart who had a studio and annual exhibition there. A century ago, his watercolours fetched as much as 25 guineas each when they were sold at Plymouth.

Writer Compton Mackenzie lived for a time at Gunwalloe and lodged for a while with the Vicar of Cury, paying him £1 a week for his keep, not including washing or wine. Sir Henry Irving, his son and other actors visited the area and stayed at Porthoustock, appreciating the quiet atmosphere of the cove, in contrast to their busy London lives. It was the ever-increasing arrival of tourists which probably contributed most to the gradual changes on the Lizard, as the 19th century slowly advanced into the twentieth.

At the turn of the century, the Italian engineer Marconi chose Poldhu Cove as the most suitable site for his early wireless experiments. As progress was made, the radio transmission station was visited by engineers from all over the world, and real foreigners were coming to live and work here. From this tiny, insignificant cove, the first faint signals were sent across the Atlantic in December 1901, to a jubilant Marconi waiting in Newfoundland. It was here that the tragic news of the loss of the *Titanic* on her maiden voyage in 1912 was received; and a message sent from here to a liner in mid-Atlantic led to the arrest of the murderer, Crippen.

With the outbreak of war in 1914, many of the young men left the farms and fishing coves to fight for their country. With them went many of the farm horses which were rounded up for inspection and selection by veterinary officers. For both men and horses, the bomb-scarred, muddy battlefields of France were a far cry from the green fields and gentle climate of the Lizard.

Bonython became the headquarters of Mullion Royal Navy Air Station, and airships became a familiar sight as they flew from here on anti-submarine patrols of the Channel. Even so, German U-boats came in very close to the Lizard shores, one sinking the steamer *Cape Finistere* in November 1917, just close to the Manacles Buoy. There was only one survivor, a negro found clinging to a crate of wet and indignant chickens.

A month later, a 4,000-ton steamer, the *Volnay*, carrying luxury items, was sunk in Porthallow Bay; she was either torpedoed or hit a mine, but the crew escaped. A strong easterly wind conveniently blew for several days, bringing most of the cargo inshore. The fishermen, unable to launch any of their boats through the debris, had to content themselves with fishing from the shore for several more days. This was just before a wartime Christmas; the crates were found to contain coffee, tea, butter, cigarettes and tinned meat.

When the war was over, life on the Lizard slowly returned to the old ways and old customs. There were a few more cars, but for the majority, who had never travelled more than a few miles in any direction, one short train journey would have been enough of an adventure to last a lifetime.

Lady Clara Vyvyan often described the Lizard countryside and the people who were close to her heart.

> I found a man', she wrote 'who goes about his business without haste or worry, appreciating as he works, the incomparable riches of the Lizard country, the variant rocks and the good earth, the sound of rooks in elms, wild birds and flowers, trees and boulders, earth bound relics of antiquity and household implements of many generations, preserving the ancient values that he will hand on to his children.

The timeless quality of the Lizard attracts everyone, whether sailor, fisherman or those content to wander along little used paths to discover quiet wooded valleys, prehistoric encampments or sheltered fishing coves.

The wealth of early photographic and illustrative material for Cornish history brings to life stories of shipwrecks and heroic lifeboat rescues, of communities scraping a living from fishing or farming, of ancient customs and famous local characters. I hope I have captured Bygone Helston and the Lizard in this miscellany of old photographs – just look carefully, for much of it is still here today.

Porthleven

1. The busy harbour at Porthleven in 1910. A merchant vessel unloads its cargo and numerous fishing boats are in port.

2. Photographed c. 1880, these neatly dressed young boys, perhaps on their way home from school, sit in an inshore fishing boat on the harbour and dream of being fishermen and lifeboatmen. On the other hand, they could be playing truant, or 'minching' as the Cornish say.

3. Looking down Fore Street to Porthleven harbour, perhaps on a Sunday. The children have their best clothes on and the fishing fleet is in.

4. In the 19th century Porthleven had a large fishing fleet, some travelling to the Scottish herring fishery each year. Not surprisingly there were also boatbuilding yards employing much local labour.

5. During the Great War, when there was an acute manpower shortage, these five Porthleven fishermen went back to work—all were aged over seventy.

Helston

6. Cunnack's Tannery in October 1883. The man wearing the black top hat is proprietor George James Cunnack, who died in 1911 at the age of 88.

7. Thatched cottages in Wendron Street, Helston, c. 1900. The shop in the foreground offers 'Pure Ices' for sale.

8. C. C. Hoadley, the founder of a firm of veterinary surgeons established in Helston for over a century since 1878. Twenty years later, he was joined by assistant Alfred Head who later married his daughter. Their son joined the practice in the 1930s and their grandson is continuing the line today.

9. Possibly one of the Ruberry brothers riding a penny-farthing bicycle at the turn of the century. One J. A. Ruberry cycled daily from Porthleven to Poldhu to work on such a bicycle.

10. Over 50 bicycles and cyclists accompanied by a vast crowd of onlookers pose outside the Grylls Memorial in Helston. In the late 19th century the town boasted a very popular cycling club known as the 'One and All'.

11. A very early Flora Day photograph. All dressed in their finest clothes, the gentry of Helston pose outside Penhellis in 1883.

12. Sir William Treloar (centre foreground) was Lord Mayor of London in 1907; his father had been a Helston merchant. In May 1907, Sir William returned to take part in the Flora Day celebrations. He watched the early morning dance from the steps of the *Angel Hotel* and, suitably clad, he took part in the mid-day dance.

13. At a presentation made in front of the Grylls Memorial Sir William Treloar received donations for a charity he had launched to aid crippled children.

14. During the day Sir William received the Freedom of Helston at the Guildhall.

HELSTON FLORA DAY. MAY 8th 1908. N°3.

15. Crowds watching the mid-day dance on Flora Day 1908, as the dancers approach the Guildhall, decorated for the occasion with traditional greenery. The market stall, one of many in the town on Flora Day, offers baskets of appetising apples and other fruit.

16. In May 1910 the Furry Dance was postponed out of respect for the late King. The proclamation of King George V was made by the Mayor of Helston from the steps of the Guildhall.

17. Unlike Flora Day in 1886, which was completely cancelled out of respect for two prominent townswomen who had died, the King's death only resulted in a postponement. The Furry Dance finally took place on a cold and blustery day in July 1910.

18.   The new Helston steam fire engine was christened 'Flora' at a ceremony at the bottom of Coinagehall Street on Friday 25 February 1910.

19.   The townspeople of Helston quietly watching the fire brigade fighting a fire at the Alpha Boarding Establishment whilst a man appears to be falling head first from the roof. However it was a carefully-planned demonstration with the new 45-foot extending ladder in use.

Gweek

20.   Until the 1930s, Gweek was a very busy port. This topsail schooner was one of many which came upriver with timber, charcoal, limestone and grain. Gweek was also the departure point for local people seeking new lives in the colonies. In this carefully-arranged study, c. 1890, crewmen, labourers, carters, quayside dwellers and dog are all keen to be in the picture.

21. The larger vessel used to bring Scandinavian timbers right up the river, after the goods were offloaded from much larger sailing ships. At low tide, it is difficult to imagine how some of the sailing schooners managed to reach so far inland.

22. Mr. Courtis's boot and shoe van paying a call in Gweek sometime before 1898.

Mawgan ~ in ~ Meneage

23.   On a very wet day in December 1922 Sir Henry Maybury declared this road, Gweek Drive, open to the public. This new road from Mawgan Cross to Gweek made access from the Lizard so much easier.

24.   Ponsuntuel Lodge on the Trelowarren estate in 1895 with estate workers and their families, namely William and Janie Rowe, William and Susan Skewes, Tommy Rowe and Ethel Skewes, Emma Gentler and William Choak.

25.   Rock Cottage at Gear Bridge in
1897, built on a large slab of rock.
During the Civil War, Royalist Captain
Hannibal Bogans made a last stand
here, positioning his men around the
narrow bridge. His men fled when a
vast Parliamentary army approached.
Many were later cornered on the cliffs
at Coverack, and threw themselves
into the sea. Captain Bogans escaped.

26.   Carabone Lodge at Trelowarren,
decorated to welcome Sir Courtney
Vyvyan home after the siege of Mafeking.

27. Trelowarren House in the 1890s, when it was the home of Sir Vyell and Lady Vyvyan. In 1752 Charles Lyttleton wrote that although the site of Trelowarren was 'wild and dreary', he was satisfied with his accommodation there. During the 18th and 19th centuries many improvements were made to both the house and gardens.

28. During alterations to the gardens at Trelowarren House Sir Vyell Vyvyan moved his sundial from its position elsewhere in the grounds to a place in the quadrangle. He is seen here with his wife and seems to be inspecting the finished result.

29. Lady Clara Vyvyan, Sir Courtney's second wife, seen here in her bronze silk wedding dress. An exceptional woman, she was a traveller and writer. Nearly 60 years ago she journeyed to the Klondyke with two Indian guides, and her book *Down the Rhone on Foot* describes a 400-mile walk she undertook at the age of 67.

30. Philip Choak was a cowman at Trelowarren for many years, seen here in the 1920s with a rather splendid motorcycle.

31. Charles Rundle, a gamekeeper at Trelowarren, with his dogs.

32. Tremayne quay was built for a proposed visit by Queen Victoria in 1846, but in the event her visit was cancelled. In 1921, the Prince of Wales arrived at the quay to be greeted by Sir Courtney Vyvyan, and was said to have been most impressed by the walk through the woods.

33. 'Crying the Neck' at Trelowarren, 1930. At the end of harvest a large sheaf, or 'neck', of corn was tied with ribbon and decorated with flowers. After a brief celebration, followed by croust and cider or a barn dance on larger farms, the 'neck' was taken to the farmhouse where it remained until the following year's harvest.

St Martin ~ in ~ Meneage

34. The Express horse bus which operated between Manaccan, St Martin and Helston. The young man (centre back), Mr. Willie Jenkin, still lives at St Anthony where he has been the church organist, bellringer and churchwarden for over 50 years.

Manaccan

35. Mr. and Mrs. Christopher Oates farmed Rosuic on the edge of Goonhilly Downs. This splendid photograph was taken about 1870 by Mr. R. Preston of Penzance who claimed to be photographer to the Prince and Princess of Wales.

36. Christopher Oates's son William examining a binder at harvest time in 1898.

37. Dog carts were quite a common sight in remote rural areas, handy transport for milk churns and the like. Kit Oates however is trying to persuade his collie to give the Jack Russell a ride round the farmyard.

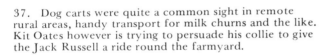

38. The kitchen at Rosuic Farm in the 1930s. Something is cooking on the traditional range or 'slab' as it is called, the all-important tea caddy is on the shelf and a dressed turkey is on the table waiting to be cooked.

39. Mr. G. Walter Jevons, a lesser-known Victorian artist and rather eccentric character, outside his cottage at Rosuic in 1891.

40. The *New Inn*. These three young lads would say the outside has changed very little if they saw it today. The sign tells visitors to 'Try our Tea Gardens' and the way to the 'Refreshment Room'. Accommodation was also available on 'moderate terms'.

Helford

41. Low tide on the Helford in 1912. The quiet solitude, a perfect backdrop for smugglers and pirates who had, in the past, given the river the name 'Stealford'. Yet tourists were already visiting this lovely river and 30 years earlier a newspaper had reported that as many as five yachts had been seen there on one summer's day.

42. Penkestle, Helford, a typical Cornish cottage described in a journal of 1880. The traveller wrote 'we came to the village of Helford. Roses bloomed over most of the cottage windows and fuchsias overtopped the houses. It was a picture of peace and flowers'.

43. Calm Helford creek, just downstream of the *Shipwrights' Arms*. Yet in the 17th century it was a busy little port with ships loading tin, fish and fertiliser, and no doubt contraband was landed here to be concealed in the thick walls of the inn.

44. Bosahan was built in 1882 for Mr. (later Sir) Arthur Pendarves Vivian, a traveller, big game hunter and writer. Many hunting trophies adorned the walls, whilst tropical plants intermingled with indigenous shrubs in the grounds. In 1956 it was demolished and 'no more will Bosahan's great bells ring out the passing hours over woodland and water'.

45. Looking from Gillan towards the church at St Anthony. The church is said to have been built by two Norman knights who came safely ashore here after being shipwrecked. Curiously enough, the tower is built of Norman stone.

46.   Small fishing boats on the beach at Bosahan in 1912. These traditional luggers with dipping lugsails provided an adequate living for an inshore fisherman and his family.

Porthallow

47. The sign over the door advertises *The Inn* at Porthallow and in smaller lettering *Five Pilchards*. Mr. Southey, the landlord, sits impressively in his jingle whilst other members of his family watch the camera. The other board on the far left of the building informs us that S. J. Southey is licensed to let a horse and trap on hire, boats for pleasure and fishing purposes.

48. Tom Smitheram of Porthallow was a fisherman. He was also an expert dowser and his services were in great demand all over the Lizard peninsula. Not only could he detect water with his hazel twig, but could judge accurately the depth at which a good source would be found.

49. Unloading maize and bran from the 40-ton *Industry* into carts waiting to take the sacks to Porthallow mill. To the right 'dowser' Tom Smitheram is going out fishing in his lugger, the *Katie*.

50. March 1891 brought sleet and snow driving in from the east. The *Bay of Panama* stripped to bare poles struck the coast near Porthallow and rapidly filled with water. Many were washed overboard, others took to the rigging and froze to death. The 17 survivors later walked to Falmouth in heavy snow, anxious to reach the Sailor's Home.

51. In the Great Blizzard of 1891, Joe James walked to Falmouth with news of the wreck of the *Bay of Panama* for the ship's agents. During the Great War he was nearly tricked into painting the Manacle Reef with whitewash as a navigational aid. Forever afterwards he was known as Manacle Joe.

52. Artist Henry Scott Tuke (centre) aboard his floating studio. The lad on the left is Jack Rollings who appeared in many of Tuke's paintings. He dived for the first time on the *Bay of Panama* wreck. Tuke watched Jack working as he sketched the *Mohegan* wreck and wrote that he sometimes earned as much as £10 a week salvaging.

53. *Arabella*, a 16-foot lugger, was built at Mylor in 1917. Named after the owner's daughter, she was an efficient working boat. It is reputed that she once carried 17 people across Falmouth Bay to see the Naval fleet. A television film was made of her restoration in 1981. In this photograph fisherman Tripp has just caught a thresher shark.

54. An exceptionally fine photograph of Porthallow taken at the turn of the century. Sheep graze on the hilly fields on the edge of the cove, seine boats wait on the sandy beach as yet unspoiled by stones from the quarry workings. A picture of contentment.

55. Porthallow regatta in 1937. People crowd on the beach for this popular event and Sunbeam yachts have come over from Falmouth for the day.

56. Cider making at Pengarrock. Sampson Hocking is in the foreground. The horse is turning the stone to crush the apples. The pulp is then put between layers of straw called a cheese, and pressed. The juice is then left in a barrel for a year. Naturally fermented apple juice without sugar or yeast is all that is necessary for a good brew of scrumpy.

St Keverne

57. The liner *Mohegan* left London bound for Australia on Thursday, 13 October 1898 with 153 passengers and crew on board. The following evening, with a cold easterly wind blowing, the vessel struck on the rocks of the outer Manacle Reef and sank in less than 20 minutes. Soon there was little to be seen other than the masts and funnel, as this rather blurred photograph reveals.

58. Villagers worked from Sunday until Tuesday in heavy rain, to prepare the mass grave 13-feet wide, 19-feet long and 10-feet deep, for the victims of the *Mohegan* wreck. The rain eased on the Tuesday morning with glimpses of sunshine when the funeral took place. Many villagers attended the service and were stunned to learn that 106 had perished in the wreck.

59. St Keverne church tower has always been an important landmark to vessels anxious to avoid the Manacle Rocks, hence their original name Maen Eglos or Church Rocks. The tower was rebuilt after it was destroyed by lightning in 1770. In 1893 the church underwent a major renovation employing many local skilled craftsmen, seen here carrying the tools of their trades.

60. Pentecost's horse bus 'Telegraph' returning from Helston. St Keverne
boasted another horse bus, Tripp's 'Fairy'. Both services had their own loyal
passengers. It was said that passengers on one bus did not dare change to the
other for fear of being ill-wished. One did, his cow became ill and he had to
seek help from Tamsin Bligh, the Helston witch.

61. After his Flora Day visit to Helston in May 1907, Sir William Treloar spent the following day at St Keverne where he opened the new peal of bells in the church tower. He is seen here with other members of his party and villagers in St Keverne Square.

62. 'Maudie', the old steam boiler and threshing set at Tregonning, in the early part of the Great War. Young Miriam Moyle (nee Martin) is more interested in the photographer, under the watchful eye of her father, farmer Johnny Martin.

63. Frank Curnow (right) had been cutting corn with a binder and team of horses at Trenoweth in 1928.

64. With the long days work over, young William Curnow takes two of the team back to their stables for a feed and well-earned rest.

65. Lanarth, once home of John Sandys, who in 1702 was blown across to France with several other St Keverne and Coverack folk when his boat ran into a sudden storm as they were returning from Falmouth. It was at the time of England's war with France, but their Breton kinsmen treated them kindly and they returned home safely.

66. A group of retired staff from the Lanarth estate, photographed in November 1924. From left to right, Mr. Thomas Jose, Mrs. Luke Martin, Mrs. Gurd, Mr. Luke Martin.

Porthoustock

67.   The coastguard watch-house at Manacle Point, from where a constant check was kept on the dangerous and submerged Manacle Reef. This photograph was taken in 1926, just before the site fell victim to the extended quarry workings.

68.   Some of the rocks in the dreaded Manacle Reef. This treacherous reef extends a mile and a half seaward and over two miles in width. Only a few of the largest rocks break the surface at high tide and each is individually named. Keeping well clear of the reef, a paddle steamer takes trippers to one of the coves.

69. James Hill, a fisherman, helped to rescue 50 people from the wreck of the *John* in 1855. When the lifeboat was provided at Porthoustock, he joined the crew and became the coxswain. In 1898, at the age of 63, he received the RNLI silver medal for his part in the rescue of survivors from the *Mohegan*.

70. Porthoustock was gaily decorated in 1886 when the new lifeboat arrived. She had to be drawn through an immense quantity of seaweed thrown up by easterly gales. As the boat was named *Charlotte*, she glided off her carriage and into the surf accompanied by cheers and applause from the crowd, whilst the village band played 'Rule Britannia'.

71. James Cliff bought the old lifeboat when the *Charlotte* arrived on station. Later, he used it as the roof for a tiny cottage he built at the top of Porthoustock beach.

72. The *James Stevens* is hauled out of Porthoustock lifeboathouse on 9 May 1907. The coxswain, James Henry Treloar Cliff, cousin to Sir William Treloar, stands in the bow. Many of the Lord Mayor's party were treated to a somewhat choppy trip round the bay—and most were seasick.

73. A steamship loading stone from the quarries in the 1930s, as can be seen from the dust rising from the hold as the stone pours out of the hoppers. Steamers of up to 500 tons could load here in under an hour, whilst barges of 50 tons have been loaded in less than 10 minutes.

74. St Keverne quarries had been worked in a small way by locals, but it was Mr. Sidney Davey of Bochym who was responsible for their development after 1896. The loading pier was constructed to facilitate loading the stone into vessels, to be delivered by sea to ports all around the coast.

75. A trio of quarrymen with the tools of their trade—Tommy Downing, Joe Peters and Herman Dudley.

Coverack

76.   Roskilly's shop and post office was a real village emporium supplying most of the village's needs. It was rumoured that the room beneath the shop, overlooking Coverack harbour, was used for smuggling.

77. Most of the coves were equipped with a rocket apparatus, operated by volunteers, which was often of great use in getting a line on board a stricken vessel when a lifeboat could not be launched. It was invented by a Helston man, Henry Trengrouse, after he witnessed the appalling wreck of the *Anson* in 1807, when many were drowned close to shore.

78.   The crew of the Coverack lifeboat who went to the aid of the German barque *Pindos*, driven ashore in 1910. Despite bad weather conditions the entire crew was saved. The lifeboat coxswain John Corin (centre) received the RNLI silver medal.

79.   The happy crew of the *Pindos* leaving for the Sailors' Home in Falmouth. The Kaiser decided to award the coxswain John Corin a gold watch, but agreed instead to the coxswain's request for a financial reward for his crew. Over 50 years later a crewman from the *Pindos* wrote 'To Mr. John Corin, I owe the fact I am still alive'.

80. The *Heather Belle* brought coal to Coverack on a regular basis. The coal was sold on the quayside for 18s. a ton. On one such voyage in 1922, she was caught in an easterly gale at the height of a spring tide and parted her moorings. This first photograph shows the stricken vessel taking a pounding from the stormy seas.

81. A message was sent to her sister ship at Gweek. Both crews worked hard to secure the vessel with hawsers and chain cables, but she broke free again, damaging the quay. This second photograph shows the continuing gale with only the *Heather Belle's* boat still on her mooring.

82. A glorious summer's day between the wars. There was an increasing demand for holiday accommodation and the new *Coverack Bay Hotel* had been built, but it was a temperance hotel.

83. Any farming at this time was labour-intensive, as can be seen here at Treliever in 1930. As many as 14 or 15 men were employed for threshing, including one man to carry the water for the steam engine.

Goonhilly

84. Believing that standing stones were erected over a 'pot of gold', some earlier inhabitants had toppled the Dry Tree Menhir. In June 1927, Col. Serecold and Col. Sir Courtney Vyvyan arranged for the menhir to be re-erected by the Porthoustock quarrymen. Sir Courtney sponsored the event and Col. Serecold provided the beer.

Kugger

85. The quiet lane leading from Kugger to Goonhilly Downs, used once by robbers and wreckers making their way to the lonely crofts up on the downs, said to be the haunt of thieves and murderers.

86. A wide junction in the tiny hamlet of Kugger does not appear to have seen much traffic. The lane from Ruan Minor turns left for Goonhilly and straight ahead for Kennack. In the 1820s a respectable young milliner's apprentice rode these lanes on horseback, not carrying hats in the hat boxes but contraband landed in the nearby coves.

Kennack Sands

87. A solitary and overdressed holidaymaker lifts her skirts to paddle at lonely Kennack Sands in the summer of 1908. Just five years earlier, a coastguard spotted three negroes and two white stowaways being put ashore here from the steamship *Pawhatten* and benevolently directed them to Cadgwith.

88. Kennack Sands between the wars when more and more people were discovering the remoter corners of the Lizard. It was here pirate Captain Avery was said to have buried 12 boxes of treasure in the late 17th century. People have searched for it unsuccessfully and many have spent a fortune doing so.

Ruan Minor

89. A farmer stands on the bridge at Poltesco mill c. 1870. Only one donkey is harnessed to the cart, a second is on a leading rein. The donkey on the left has a tiny foal standing behind her. In this rocky coastal area, donkeys were in common use, for both legal and illegal purposes.

90. Poltesco mill and farm in the luxuriant valley near Ruan Minor. This early photograph captures a way of life which, to workers in the black industrial areas of Britain of the time, would have been considered a relatively idyllic existence.

91. Poltesco cove once buzzed with life as the Serpentine Works produced shop-front panels, ornate fireplace surrounds and other larger items beyond the scope of the cottage workers. These were shipped directly from the cove.
The works closed down in 1897 when, it is thought, an uninsured ship carrying a valuable cargo of their goods sank
with great financial loss.

92. Interested onlookers watching the wheelwright at work outside his workshop in Ruan Minor. The house on the
right, beyond the school wall, was Michell's the Bakers, renowned for its splits and traditional saffron buns.

93. Tommy Daw always met the motorised mail van on the Helston to The Lizard road at his hut by the turning to Cadgwith. The mail was transferred to his donkey shay for him to deliver to the district around Cadgwith and Ruan Minor. A popular and well-known character, he appears on countless postcards and private snapshots.

94. Mr. Morgan was a man of many parts; a shopkeeper with a rural round, and also a taxi driver. Seen here outside Nicholl's garage, he was taking these holidaymakers into Helston to catch the train. There is so much luggage in the car that one wonders where the passengers sat.

Cadgwith

95. The *Brest* left Le Havre on Saturday 6 September 1879. She carried a cargo of champagne, tobacco and raw sugar together with 130 Italian and German emigrants to America. That same evening she struck on Polberro Point between Church Cove and Cadgwith. Interestingly there are three gigs at the scene, as well as a French fishing boat.

96. A group of melancholy survivors from the *Brest* awaiting transport to the Sailors' Home in Falmouth. Many of the Italians had already survived an earlier wreck on the Mediterranean coast and not surprisingly refused to go to Falmouth by boat. Horse-drawn transport was provided for them.

97. An interesting group outside the cottages on the Todden in 1894. The couple are Henry and Ellen Jane who brought up a large family in this tiny cottage. The day's work done, there was time for a chat and to enjoy the fresh evening air.

98. Edwin Rutter, William Edward Mitchell and Jarvis Stephens outside Ship Cottage. Above the cottage doors in the background, the old bricked up window had a window painted on the bricks. Sometime before the Great War, Harry Arthur painted the *Socoa* under sail in place of the painted window.

99. The *Socoa* was bound for America when she struck the Craggan Rock in 1906. Her cargo of cement was for the rebuilding of earthquake-devastated San Francisco. In increasingly bad weather, the lifeboat made three trips, saving all the crew. The solidified cement was jettisoned and, after temporary repairs, the vessel was taken to Falmouth for a complete overhaul.

100. Ship Cottage again with Lena Stephens and Susie Arthur chatting by their doors, and Dick Exelby driving the cart. Miss Mitchell's little shop used to open at all hours, signified by a lighted candle in the window. Fishermen catching an early tide could buy their 'baccy', even at four in the morning.

101. In such a tightly-knit community as Cadgwith, the fishermen, coastguards and customs officers relied on each other for assistance in times of danger, when there was a wreck. But the fishermen were quick to deceive the customs and coastguard officers if a spot of profitable wrecking came their way.

102. The Cadgwith lifeboat, probably the *Minnie Moon*, undergoing either examination or repair on the beach. The lifeboat had to be kept in a state of readiness and, unless the repairs were of a serious nature, the lifeboatmen generally undertook the day-to-day maintenance themselves.

103. Travelling shops were a great boon to families living in the remote corners of the Lizard. Stevie Morgan, who had the village shop at Ruan Minor, also did a round with vegetables and fruit, and is seen here outside Bessie Arthur's cottage at Cadgwith.

104. John Tunnard, a leading British surrealist painter, lived in a gipsy caravan at Cadgwith from the mid-1930s until 1947. He painted to a jazz accompaniment which, it is said, influenced his abstract paintings. A popular man, seen here in 1935 playing the drums in an informal session with Ball Jane, Affie Wylie and Buller Arthur outside Dummy's loft.

Landewednack ~ The Lizard

105. *Marriners* above Landewednack Church cove was once an illegal beer shop or kiddleywink and doubtless involved in smuggling activities. A century or so ago, a document issued by parish worthies, including the Rector, threatened legal action against all villagers found in possession of stolen goods, but smuggled goods were 'excepted'.

106. Steamships regularly left Falmouth bound for Church Cove, Kynance and other coves on the Lizard peninsula. These were popular, but expensive excursions. In the 1870s, a return ticket cost 2s. 6d. Families were much larger in those days and a family ticket was £1 for 10 tickets. Photographs 106-108 were all taken on the same day. The first shows passengers being rowed ashore to the steep slipway at Church Cove.

107. Dressed in all their finery, passengers from the S.S. *Victor* disembark at the narrow cove.

108. The old tea house at Landewednack Church Cove, a favourite place with the day-trippers. A peaceful voyage from Falmouth, the excitement of being ferried ashore, followed by a mouth-watering tea in a thatched cottage with roses round the door, was undoubtedly a lovely way to spend a summer's day.

109. The rugged coastline around the Lizard can be seen to advantage here at Housel Bay, with two people taking a rest on the well-trodden cliff walk.

110. In May 1913, the *Queen Margaret*, an elegant four-masted barque carrying a cargo of wheat, was waiting for tugs to tow her round Land's End. Beating slowly back and forth, she suddenly came to a halt. Only then did the crew spot the submerged weed-covered rocks—she was stuck firmly on the Maenheere Rock.

111.   The lifeboat brought everyone safely ashore together with a barrel of rum, a pig and a cat. A farmer bought the pig, the cat went to live at the pub and no doubt the rum found a good home too. The swollen wheat split the vessel apart and she quickly disappeared.

112. The steamship *Mosel* carrying a cargo of silk, lace, calf skins, champagne, ostrich feathers and Meerschaum pipes ran onto rocks just under Lloyds Signal Station in August 1882. The noise was heard for miles, but everyone on board was saved. The wreck proved to be a highly profitable one for salvers and wreckers—often one and the same people.

113. 'The Lion's Den', formed when the roof of a cave (or hugo as the Cornish say) fell in sometime during the 19th century, and Bumble Rock on the left, are silent witnesses to an elegant four-masted barque bound for Falmouth.

114. Lizard lighthouse looking very spick and span inside the walls. The keepers were not allowed to keep livestock inside the establishment, and thus erected lean-to chicken houses outside the walls, from where the hens could range freely along the clifftops.

115. A faked photograph of the Lizard lighthouse. Its beam was not always so bright in the days when a coal fire provided the light. On one occasion a packet boat's captain noticed that the light was very low, and fired a cannon near the lighthouse to wake up the keeper.

116. Goodman's, Jose's and Matthews's serpentine workshops at The Lizard. Edwin Matthews was also a fisherman and huer, whilst Francis Jose was an official guide. Many locals supplemented their incomes from fishing by working the serpentine rock, but not all had such lavish workshops. The poster outside Edwin Matthews's workshop is advertising artist Thomas Hart's studio exhibition.

117. Squibb's Serpentine Bazaar at The Lizard displaying clocks and lighthouses expertly turned from the beautiful green and red rock which is found locally. Like many other serpentine craftsmen, Mr. Squibb was also a member of The Lizard lifeboat.

118. In March 1907 the liner *Suevic* was wrecked at The Lizard, an event which drew vast crowds to the cliffs, all fascinated by the sight of the wreck and the salvage operations.

119. Crowds assembled on the beach when salvaged wool from the wreck of the *Suevic* was sold.

120. A holidaymaker in the 1920s captured a unique scene. A collier had been stranded and its cargo jettisoned. Locals worked hard to salvage the coal as it was washed ashore. A horse pulling a heavily-laden wooden sledge takes the strain as it is led up the steep cliffside field.

121. The *Hansy* was wrecked at Penolver in November 1911. The captain's wife, son, most of the crew, a dog and a cat were hauled up the cliff-face to safety. The lifeboatmen rescued the captain and two crewmen. The following day a pig and two goats were discovered alive in the wreckage.

122. The *Adolph Vinnen* was on her maiden voyage in ballast to load coal. In severe headwinds, she was driven ashore 70 yards off Bass Point in February 1923. A large crowd had already assembled and 17 crewmen were saved by breeches buoy. In this picture one crew member has reached safety and is drinking something warming after his ordeal.

123. The captain, officers and steward stayed on board the *Adolph Vinnen*, but during the night heavy seas continually swept through the decks and they had to take to the rigging. In this dramatic photograph, one man can just be seen in the forward rigging, whilst another is swinging above the waves towards a helper on the cliff-face.

124. Until the new toll road was constructed, the only proper approach to Kynance was by way of the double hedge path. Over a century ago authoress Mrs. Craik walked to Kynance through the fields and returned by this path, enjoying a beautiful sunset at the end of a memorable day.

125. An attractively-posed photograph of harvest time at The Lizard, taken in 1870.

Kynance

126.   Goats were frequently grazed on the cliffs around the coast. This flock presumably belonged to the isolated community at Kynance, dominated by Thomas's Private Hotel. The tide is high and the sea quite rough, which could explain the absence of visitors.

127.   Elegantly dressed Victorian ladies and gentlemen making their way down to view the natural splendour of Kynance Cove, with its dramatic rocks and magnificent caves only accessible for two hours each side of low tide.

Mullion

128. Mullion Cove in the 1860s. A solitary thatched cottage stands between the new lifeboathouse and net loft.
Seine boats and smaller fishing boats drawn up suggest the weather is unsuitable for fishing. Recent gales have
thrown seaweed onto the beach, and the fishermen's loss is the farmers' gain, as they load the cart in the foreground
with seaweed, a valuable fertiliser.

129. Mullion's first lifeboat, the
Daniel D. Draper, was delivered to
the cove in September 1867, having
been launched at Penzance three
days earlier. The crew is seen here
with some of the village notables,
including two well-dressed ladies
sitting in the boat and Parson
Harvey leaning on the stern, clad in
clerical black and top hat.

130. William Mundy, a lifelong fisherman, was the first coxswain of the lifeboat *Daniel D. Draper*. He is seen here, proudly wearing his cork lifejacket, woollen hat and traditional Lizard pattern knit-frock. In April 1872, his fishing boat sank off Porthleven, taking with it William aged 58, two of his sons, Joel 25, and Henry 13, and John Williams aged twenty.

131. A legend in her own lifetime was Miss Mary Mundy who kept the *Old Inn* until the 1880s. Mentioned in the earliest guide books, her homemade teas were said to be 'worthy of the gods'. Visited by many important people including Lord Randolph Churchill and immortalised in a poem, she will always be remembered in the area.

132. The *Old Inn* at Mullion was a favourite port of call for the local fishermen, whatever time they came ashore, wet, cold and tired. When this photograph was taken, c. 1900, Orlando Bosustow was land-lord; he remained so until 1926.

133. Mullion harbour under construction in 1887. Before this date, fishing boats were drawn up the beach each day. In settled weather they were anchored offshore with a watchman on the beach. If the weather suddenly changed, the fishermen spent a long night working together to get all the boats ashore.

134. Henry George in 1897 when he was 78 years old. Like many others on the Lizard, he made a living from the sea by any opportunity which presented itself. Fisherman, huer, wrecker and smuggler—Henry George was all of these.

135. Mullion church as it was in Parson Harvey's time. Not only did he write the famous Mullion 'Gull' book as it is known but physically worked on the restoration of the church.

136. Mark Bray and his family outside their cottage at Parc an Sheta in Mullion c. 1900.

137. Many renowned artists came to paint in the villages around the Lizard, finding inspiration in the deserted villages and tiny fishing coves. These two sitting under their umbrellas in a cave at Mullion are unidentified.

138. Artist Charles Napier Hemy, seen here in his studio c. 1900, had a deep love for the sea and the Cornish fishing community. His illustrations for Mrs. Craik's timeless book about the Lizard captured and complimented her word-picture of the places she visited and the people she met.

Poldhu

139. Marconi and his assistant Kemp working on their wireless experiments at Poldhu. The first signals were sent across the Atlantic in December 1901.

140.   In July 1903 the Prince and Princess of Wales visited the Poldhu station. Accompanying Their Majesties were Prince Alexander of Teck, General Lord Grenfell, Lady Falmouth and Mr. Marconi. The Princess also found time to visit a serpentine workshop on the Lizard. Seeing an attractive item for sale, she entered to enquire the price. She was told, 'I dunno m'dear. My wife is the boss, and she's gone gallivanting to see the Princess'.

Cury

141.   The Bonython family name appears in local records from the late 13th century. Bonython House dates in part from c. 1600. It was the home of Captain Richard Bonython who emigrated to America in 1631. In the Great War, Bonython was the headquarters of Mullion R.N. Air Station and from here airships flew on anti-submarine patrols over the Channel.

142.   In the Spring of 1934 Sir Alan Cobham's Flying Circus came to Bonython. Captain Percival Phillips, seen here with his young son, flew the Mongoose-engined Avro and was a founder of the Cornish Aviation Company.

143.   This Handley Page Clive 22-seater airliner was a popular attraction. A 20-minute trip cost 7s. 6d.—for most locals more than a day's pay. One St Keverne man who did not manage to get a flight at Cury, cycled to Helford, crossed the ferry and cycled to Mawnan Smith to be first in the queue when the Circus visited that village.

144. Bochym has had a chequered history: once a Royalist refuge, the original house was destroyed by Cromwell. After the Civil War the mansion was rebuilt with terraced gardens. Sometime after 1825 Stephen Davey restored and extended the house and gardens. Photographs 144/147 show the house at its best. This first exterior view was taken in the 1880s.

145. The comfortable drawing room at Bochym, complete with a specimen salmon in a glass case.

146.   The conservatory full of lush greenery and exotic plants.

147.   The family and guests leaving Bochym for Flora Day 1890.

Gunwalloe

148. Gunwalloe church on the very edge of the sea. In the winter gales it is not uncommon for spray to fly completely over the church. The man on the beach with his horse and cart is probably collecting sand, but he might be doing a spot of wrecking at the same time.

149. The 1910 All Souls Day procession at Gunwalloe with Father Wason, the villagers carrying flowers to cast on the sea in memory of the countless thousands who have lost their lives around this coast. It was another Vicar of Gunwalloe who said he was 'conscious of something deeply spiritual there, I've many times felt surrounded by the departed'.